MIND

—over—

mutter

MIND

—over—

mutter

199 Practical Tips
for Giving Great Presentations

Barry F. Mitsch

PYRAMIS PRESS

PUBLISHED BY PYRAMIS PRESS

MIND OVER MUTTER: 199 PRACTICAL TIPS FOR GIVING GREAT
PRESENTATIONS. Copyright © 2009 by Barry F. Mitsch.
All rights reserved. Printed in the United States. No part of this
book may be used or reproduced in any manner whatsoever
without written permission except in the case of brief quotations
embodied in critical articles and reviews. For information or
additional copies, please address The Pyramid Resource Group, Inc.
1020 Southhill Drive, Suite 150, Cary, North Carolina, 27513.

REVISED EDITION

Designed by Brian M Johnson, LOUDEST ink LLC

ISBN 10: 0-615-32067-8
ISBN 13: 978-0-615-32067-0

Acknowledgements for the Revised Edition

I want to acknowledge all of the organizations who have allowed me to work with intelligent and inspiring people over these many years. Whether it was a scientist, an engineer, an accountant, a new manager, an MBA student, or even a teenager, I have always gained much from working with each and every person. They are the source of many ideas in this book and the reason why I continue to want to help people master this skill. And special acknowledgement to the continued patience and support provided by my wife and business partner, DJ Mitsch. She never stops reminding me that teaching is one of my gifts and something that I need to share each and every day.

Introduction to the Revised Edition

"Mind Over Mutter" has been one of those pleasant surprises that often makes me smile. I have received nothing but great feedback and this motivated me to update the book and add more useful content. I enjoy watching folks who attend my workshops and seminars browse through the book and nod their heads in agreement when they see a tip that hits home.

Many of the new tips come from readers and workshop participants. While very little has changed in presentation strategy and delivery, I often come across some useful tips that will help the business presenter. The most dynamic changes in presentation capability continue in the software world. I admit that in the first edition of the book I was reluctant to specifically name "PowerPoint" and opted for the general term "presentation software." While there are many software packages available, PowerPoint has become so ubiquitous in the business world that it is silly not to refer to it by name.

The introduction of PowerPoint 2007 has provided speakers with access to more graphic power that may or may not be a good thing. I have not added much about the expanded capabilities of PowerPoint because I always caution presenters about wasting too much time on slick graphics in your day-to-day presentations. But I do refer to some resources that will be helpful. Technology has not lessened the importance of being able to deliver a powerful verbal message that is concise and organized.

Giving presentations does not have to be a difficult task. I hope this book of tips will help you keep it simple so you can speak from your heart and be successful with any audience. Good luck!

Barry F. Mitsch
CARY, NORTH CAROLINA
September, 2009

Introduction

I entered graduate school at the University of North Carolina in 1981 following a two-year stint in the Peace Corps. A requirement for a Master's Degree in Environmental Sciences was a public defense of my master's research. I dreaded that event from the very day I learned of its necessity for graduation. Did I really want the degree that badly? Wouldn't it be easier to just get a job? I was faced with the decision of dropping out of school or facing my fear. Over twenty years later, I still have the fear but have learned many skills and strategies that can benefit any professional who needs to give presentations as part of their work or civic life.

Facing my fear led to a local Toastmasters Club in Chapel Hill. Toastmasters was the starting point on my learning curve and I recommend that organization to anyone looking for immediate and consistent help with public speaking. The skills I learned in Toastmasters led to the successful completion of my Master's Degree and also contributed to my being hired by a technical services company after graduation. I got the job not because of a superior resume, but because of a superior presentation that I gave to the company during the interview process.

The benefits of being a proficient speaker were obvious. As I entered the work force, I noticed there were many people who hated giving presentations. And even when they spoke, they were less than inspiring and often very ineffective. There was a dire need for a practical approach to developing and delivering effective presentations.

Eventually my burgeoning interest in this topic led to the development of a workshop I called "Technically Speaking." The workshop created many speaking opportunities, led to the production of a video-based companion program, got me involved in distance learning using satellite and video-conferencing technology, and provided the opportunity to work with hundreds of professionals in group and private sessions.

I have accumulated an immense amount of practical knowledge about giving presentations and wanted to create a way to share that with as many people as possible. I also wanted to create a means for learning even more about this essential skill from people working in diverse fields around the globe. So my hope is that this little book will be a valuable resource for professionals who deliver presentations in all arenas of business and civic life, and that people will share their practical tips for inclusion in later editions.

Barry F. Mitsch
CARY, NORTH CAROLINA
October, 2003

How to use this book

One of the motivations for compiling Mind Over Mutter was that I got tired of reading book after book on presentations skills that were just repeating essentially the same concepts. Very rarely would I learn something new. So rather than pontificate for a couple of hundred pages, I wanted to let readers get to the bottom line as fast as possible.

So, if you are a fast reader, take less than 30 minutes and read the book cover to cover. You can read it over lunch, during your breaks, or sitting in an airport. Highlight the tips you find useful for future reference.

If you need quick ideas, use the index in the back of the book to find information on just about any topic dealing with presentations.

If you have a presentation coming up, use the book to help you get prepared, review your presentation content, and prepare to deliver your best performance. And then pass it on!

199 Practical Tips

Getting Started

1
There are no rules

In my opinion, the only rule that applies to presentation skills—and public speaking—is that "there are no rules." Everyone has different strengths and weaknesses and some people can get away with things others should never attempt. The key is to optimize your individual strengths. Use your God-given ability to its highest level. Find out what works for you and what doesn't. Constantly observe other speakers and try to adopt styles and techniques that fit your personality.

2
The critical first step

A successful presentation must have a clearly defined purpose or objective. There are essentially two types of objectives. An informative objective focuses on what you want people to KNOW; a persuasive objective focuses on what you want people to DO. Before you begin to develop content for a presentation, define a clear objective.

There is always information

3

Every presentation will have information regardless if it is intended to be informative or persuasive. Focus on what specific outcome is desired to determine if your presentation is strictly informative or persuasive. There are very few "purely" informative presentations. We usually have some action that is desired, even if the action is not immediate.

Crafting an objective

4

The easiest way to develop an objective for a presentation is to answer one or both of these questions:
1) Why am I giving this presentation?
2) What do I want to have happen as a result of the presentation?

Make it simple

5

Make your objective short and sweet. Try to capture it in one or two sentences. The objective of my presentation is to...

6   *Measure the outcome*

The best objectives are those that can be measured with an outcome. How many people signed up for my offering? How many people followed the procedure I discussed? Was my proposal accepted? You will have a more concise objective when you can tie it to a measurable outcome.

7   *The critical second step*

The purpose of any presentation is to meet the needs of an audience—it's not about the speaker! Once you have a clear objective, you must analyze the audience in terms of as many factors as possible—knowledge, receptivity to your topic, experience, decision-making power, influence, age, sex, context of your presentation with others, and much more.

Customizing a business presentation 8

Talk to colleagues who have presented to
this client in the past and ask them what
worked and what did not work. Ask about
the conference room or meeting location and
understand any logistical challenges. Do a dry
run for a small group of colleagues and ask for
input and suggestions for improvement.

Use the internet 9

Use the internet to research corporate
information prior to any presentation to a new
client and/or company. Every company has
a web-site that usually includes press releases
and current information that will be useful
in customization. Ask permission to
use their logo to customize any slides or
handout material.

Customizing for a conference 10

Become best friends with the conference
planner. Request a list of attendees and
contact 3-4 of them personally to discuss their

needs and expectations. Get the name of the audio-visual technician who is coordinating the conference. Also request a layout of the room where you will be speaking.

11 *More on conference presentations*

Get the agenda and note the persons and topics who will be speaking before and after you. Contact other speakers on the agenda and ask them if they can share any information they may have to help you customize your presentation

12 *Create a target plan*

A target plan consists of a clearly defined purpose or objective for the presentation coupled with an analysis of the listeners to whom you will be presenting. When you have that information clearly defined, choosing content for the presentation simply requires that you answer the question, "What content do I need to include in the presentation to meet *this* objective for *this* group of people?"

Getting people to listen 13

Most people are not great listeners; they simply have too much on their personal agendas. The best presentations overcome listening limitations by being well organized, customized to the audience, and include many "change elements" that keep people's attention.

Change elements 14

A change element can be visual or vocal, high-tech or low-tech—just something that keeps the content more interesting. Watch any television program and observe how often the screen changes. You create change elements through movement, vocal variety, visual aids, and audience interaction.

Prepare an introduction 15

If you are going to be introduced, it is best to prepare your own introduction. The introduction should answer the questions: Why this speaker? Why this subject? Why this audience? Only include information that will augment the subject of your presentation and establish your credibility for *this* specific subject being presented to *this* specific audience. This is more important than telling the audience where you are from, what schools you attended, and what your hobbies are.

16 — *A great resource*

Epson sponsors a comprehensive web site that is great for helping you with all phases of presenting. Visit www.presentersonline.com.

Formulating Content

17 — *Organization*

The oldest theories about presentations go back to the days of Aristotle. His three keys to a successful presentation are the logos, pathos, and ethos. The logos is how you organize your thoughts...it must have a logical order. Consider organizing your main points in a way that makes the most sense to your listeners.

Pathos

18

Aristotle's "pathos" relates to emotion and why it is necessary to customize presentations to appeal to the needs of a specific audience. Never forget that you are presenting for the audience and meeting their needs is critical if you want to have a successful presentation.

Ethos

19

The ethos relates to the credibility of the speaker. This is why Tip 15 is so important. Your introduction can establish your credibility, so carefully consider what the audience needs to know about you that will make you credible.

The "three pointer"

20

The best presentations have limited numbers of key points. Try to use the old "three pointer" to organize your content. First, next, last—past, present, future—problem, cause, solution. Keep the content in bite-size chunks and people will find it easier to follow and remember.

21 *Tell 'em, tell 'em, told 'em*

The oldest and simplest advice about organizing a presentation is to "tell 'em what you're gonna tell 'em (the opening), tell 'em (the body), and tell 'em what you told 'em (the closing). It works all the time.

22 *Limited numbers of key points*

While the old three-pointer is great, complex presentations often require more than three main points. But never exceed 7...it's just too much information for an audience to digest, regardless of the length of your talk. Bundle, categorize, and combine your content into themes and "chunks"...get it covered in no more than 7 main topic areas or main points. But three is better!

23 *Brainstorm the content*

The easiest way to develop a presentation quickly is to brainstorm everything you know about your topic. Start with a blank sheet of

paper and fill it up with ideas. Then simply
select content to meet your objective for
a specific audience.

Use mind mapping 24

Mind mapping is another technique to quickly
generate lots of potential content. A mind
map is a diagram that shows the relationship
of ideas. Start with your main idea in a bubble
in the middle of a sheet of paper and build it
out, idea by idea. Topics will grow and before
you know it, you will have lots of content to
draw from. There are even some mind mapping
software programs, just search the internet.

Verbal before visual 25

Many speakers begin crafting a presentation
by first developing their visual aids.
Avoid this tendency and work on the verbal
content first. Then, your visuals will more likely
be appropriate and have more impact.

26 *Story telling*

Personal stories always add power to
a presentation if they relate to your purpose.
Always look for "real-life" examples that help
you emphasize your points and add credibility
to your presentation.

27 *Start an archive of stories*

Create a special folder—electronic or paper—
where you can collect stories that relate
to your topics. Look for stories within your
company, in your industry, or in everyday life
that help spice up your presentations.

28 *Beware of technical jargon*

Jargon and acronyms can spoil a good
presentation. Unless you are 100% certain
that everyone in your audience can speak your
"language," get rid of any unfamiliar technical
terms and be sure to define any acronym at
least once before you use it.

Speaking Impromptu

Never get caught unprepared.
Many presentations are informal. For example,
you may be unexpectedly asked for
a brief project update at a monthly meeting.
Anticipate these situations and be prepared
with a concise outline (either in your mind or
written out) that will enable you to express
your key points. Any time you attend a meeting
or other event, ask yourself what topics you
might be asked to speak on...be ready!

MIND over mutter

13

Notes ‒‒

Barry F. Mitsch

Practice Techniques

30 *Practicing*

You can improve your presentation if you have time to practice it with a small group and get some feedback. In lieu of practicing with a live audience, focus on private vocal practice where you can walk through the entire presentation.

31 *Practice with your last set of visual aids and notes*

Always have a practice session that includes the final draft of any visual material and the last draft of any notes you will be using. This will help you become familiar with the tools that will be critical to your success. If you are planning an electronic presentation, practice with the equipment you will be using, especially the computer and projector.

Practice without your slides 32

One way to streamline a presentation and your visuals is by doing a practice run without the slides. You might be surprised to find that you really don't need as many slides as you thought. The more you can speak from your heart and not from slides, the more powerful you will be as a presenter.

Practice and don't stop 33

Once you feel you are ready to go, have a practice session where you do not allow yourself to stop once you have begun the presentation. Chances are you may get lost or forget a small part of your presentation and that's perfectly fine. Just don't stop, feel what its like to get lost and recover during practice. You will be more confident during the real thing.

34 *Videotaping*

Videotaping a practice presentation is one of the most powerful tools to improve your presentation style. Just about everybody owns a camcorder, you can even use your cell phone. Use video to help you become a better speaker.

35 *Audiotaping*

If you can't videotape, try recording your presentation using an iPod or simple recording device. Listening to the playback will help you improve your vocal delivery, identify some of the "fillers" you may be using such as *ah* and *um*, and also help you remember keys points by engraining them in your memory.

36 *Fast forward advantage*

One of the most powerful observational tools is to watch yourself on videotape in the "fast forward" mode. Fast forward will highlight any repetitive movements, nervous habits and distracting mannerisms that can be minimized.

Toastmasters

A great place to practice your presentation skills on an ongoing basis is at a Toastmasters Club. Check www.toastmasters.org for a club in your area.

Look for places to practice

The best way to become a better presenter is to give more presentations. If your professional life does not provide frequent opportunities, get involved in some extracurricular activities that do. Join a Toastmasters Club, become an officer in a civic club, teach a class at church or a community college, volunteer to read at a school...the possibilities are endless. The better speakers are better because they have more opportunities.

Get a buddy...or two

Presenters get better by giving more presentations...and getting constructive feedback after each presentation to find out how they can improve. How can you get this

feedback? A great way is to have your work
team attend a presentation skills workshop
together. Agree to provide each other feedback on style and content after
future presentations.

Openings

40   *A standard opening*

A fool-proof opening has three parts:
1) provide some brief background
information that serves to put everyone on
common ground;
2) state the objective or purpose of your
presentation; and
3) preview your main points.

41   *Value of previewing main points*

By previewing your main points, you help
to establish a pattern for listeners to follow.
When you tell them you will talk about points
A, B, and C, they figuratively label file folders
in their minds with points A, B, and C. As you

move from point to point in your presentation,
the preview helps them follow you with
closer attention.

Humor 42

Many speakers begin a presentation with some
humor. Humor is only effective if it relates
to the content and objective of your
presentation. Avoid using humor if it is not
relevant to your content.

Personal stories 43

A personal story often makes a great opening,
especially if it relates to the critical content of
your presentation. Keep stories short, concise,
and relative.

Quotes 44

A relevant quotation from a famous person can
grab attention. There are many internet sites
where you can search for great quotations.
Google "quotations" and you will find
a plethora of resources.

45

Setting ground rules

Your opening is also the time to set any ground rules. When will you welcome questions... anytime, after the presentation, after main parts of the presentation? Now is the time to let your audience know.

MIND over *mutter*

— —   ***Notes***

Closings

The essential closing element 46

In a business presentation, always summarize
your main points in your closing. This is where
you tell them what you told them.
Many speakers commonly overlook this
essential element.

Call for action 47

If your presentation has a persuasive objective,
the closing is the time to call for action, ask for
agreement, and get the buy in from the group.
Tell them what you need to have happen in
the closing.

Don't end with questions 48

Many speakers end their presentations by
asking for questions. If you do have a question
and answer period, always reserve the last
few minutes for yourself to close again by
summarizing your main points. Get the last
word, it's your presentation!

49 *Leave something behind*

A closing is a good time to hand out any supplementary information that may be needed for the group. It is best to have it available in the back of the room to pick up as they leave, or efficiently pass it out if the group is remaining for continued meetings or presentations.

Transitions

50 *Verbal transitions*

You can help your audience follow your presentation by providing clear verbal transitions between the elements of your talk. Transitions serve as the bridges that connect the opening, main points and closing.

51 *Transitions from opening to body*

Try these simple transitions from the opening to the body: 1) "Let's get started...the first point I want to make is..." 2)"First, let's establish the reasons for the [problem, overrun, etc.]" 3) "My first main point is…" 4) [display a visual aid] "Let's take a look at…"

Transitions from main point to main point

Try these transitions between main points: 1) "That gives you the big picture; now let's focus on some details." 2) "Now that I have outlined the features of the product, let's talk about the benefits." 3) "Those are the pros and cons of alternative A, now let's talk about alternative B."

Putting on the brakes

Transitions from the body of your talk to the conclusion are often referred to as "brake lights." Examples include: 1)"…in conclusion…" 2)"Let me summarize…" 3) "Let's pull it all together…" Use a brake light to indicate you have completed the main body of your presentation.

Vocal Skills

54 *Tape record your voice*

One of the best ways to improve your vocal skills is to record yourself while speaking in any situation. Purchase a small, hand-held tape recorder or an iPod and take it with you to every speaking engagement. Listen to yourself and ask how you can improve your vocal delivery with subtle changes in pace, pitch, and volume.

55 *Green eggs and ham*

A great place to practice vocal variety is to read children's books out loud. Some of the same speech alterations you use to make a children's book interesting can be used in a business presentation.

Better too fast than too slow 56

It's better to speak too fast than too slow;
people can process information at a very
rapid rate. However, nothing beats selective
changes in pace to emphasize keys points and
maintain interest.

Better too loud than too soft 57

Your audience must be able to hear you.
But, you can make great use of changes in
volume to emphasize key points, provide
passion, exude enthusiasm, and add polish to
your delivery.

Pausing is good 58

Researchers actually found that people
remember what is said after a pause. It helps
draw attention and can be used for emphasis
and drama. Don't be afraid to pause on
occasion to collect your thoughts and stay
on track. This can also be important before
answering a question. Give yourself a few
seconds to formulate a response.

59 *Minimize the ah's*

Most people do not realize how often they use non-words such as "ah" or "um" until they hear their voice recorded. The first step in minimizing these distracters is to be aware of their presence in your speech pattern. Invest in a recording device and listen to your presentations. Be aware of the "ahs" and work to minimize their presence.

60 *Amplification*

You will typically need a microphone for audiences greater than 40 people. But this is not always the case since it depends on the quality of the room and the acoustics. Determine if you will need amplification by doing a dry run with colleagues seated at the rear of the room to give you feedback on how well they can hear you.

The power of the voice

Remember that most of the world's greatest speeches were only heard by most people, not seen. From Winston Churchill to Martin Luther King, the great speeches are remembered because of their vocal quality, not because of superior visuals aids or body language. Work on improving your vocal power and your presentations will dramatically improve.

Using Technology

You are the best visual aid

With all the technology available for presentations, remember that YOU are still the focus of the presentation. Technology is a TOOL, not the driving force of a great presentation.

Keep the lights on

Your presentation will be more powerful in a fully lighted room. Choose technology that allows you to present without turning off lights. The newer projectors are very bright and can be used in well-lit rooms.

64 *Overhead projectors*

This somewhat obsolete piece of equipment still has some usefulness in the computer age. If you use an overhead, place your transparencies in FlipFrames™ available from 3M Company. These frames make your transparencies easy to transport, they will appear more professional on the screen, and you can use the white space on the flip sheets for notes. Just practice the "flipping" action before your presentation.

65 *Advancing slides with a computer*

There are many ways to advance slides using a computer. You can advance slides using the space bar, the page-up command, with a mouse click, or even with the roller function on the mouse. Practice using all these approaches and use the method you find most comfortable.

Number your slides

Even when using a computer, it's good to number your slides. Someone may want you to refer back to a specific slide. In PowerPoint, you can get to any slide quickly by tapping on the number key(s) for the slide and hitting the return key. If you need to get to slide #7... tap on 7, then return and you are there.

Use a "bumper" slide

67

This is a final slide that serves as a bookmark for the speaker. It can be a corporate logo, a repeat of a title slide, or simply a blank background slide. In the latest versions of PowerPoint, the screen will go black when you advance past your last slide. This is OK, but a bumper slide can serve as a better visual bookmark.

Hip-pocket slides

68

Another great use of a bumper slide is to conceal "hip-pocket" slides after the bumper. These are slides with additional information

Barry F. Mitsch

that may be needed during a Q&A session.
Know the numbers of these slides and use
Tip 66 to call for this information if needed.

69   *Use the "B" Key*

While in slide view mode, PowerPoint lets you
darken the screen by hitting the "B" key (B as
in blank). Hitting any key will bring the screen
back. This tool is a great way to bring the
audience's attention back to you, particularly in
a question and answer session.

70   *Another use of the "B" Key*

The "B" key is also useful for starting
a presentation. Get your computer set up
before your audience arrives, put your first
slide up and then press "B" to hide the
presentation. When you are ready to get
started or refer to your first slide, hit any key
and you're on your way.

The "W" Key

Just as hitting the "B" key will make the screen
go blank while in slide show mode, the "W" key
will make it go white. Don't bother with this, it
has no useful purpose! Even a lit white screen
will distract your audience.

Check the final product

A presentation that looks great on your
desktop computer often does not look as
appealing when projected on a screen.
Better to test it out on the actual equipment
you will be using.

Preventing computer lockup

There can be many reasons for a computer
locking up during a presentation. Try these
preventative tips: 1) make sure you have
enough memory, especially if you are using
complicated graphics; 2) close out any
applications not needed for the presentation;
and 3) make sure you are using the same
hardware and software that was successful in
multiple dry runs.

MIND over matter

31

Barry F. Mitsch

74   *Backup systems*

Using technology has its risks. It's a good idea to take backup copies of any presentations you might be using as well as a backup CD for any software needed for the presentation. A zip drive or memory stick can also be a useful backup tool. Make your presentation as failure proof as possible.

75   *Low-tech insurance*

Do you have a really high-tech presentation with even higher stakes attached to the outcome? Consider hiring an IT technician to be your "caddy" and give you peace of mind that the technical side of things will be handled.

76   *Send it ahead*

Consider sending your presentation files ahead to the meeting site. Communicate with a technician on-site to make sure everything is loaded on the computer you will be using and running properly. And then take a back-up copy!

Check the final product   77

It is risky to use live web interaction during a presentation. It is better to embed screen captures into your slide show. You can simulate web interaction by moving rapidly from slide to slide.

Remote mouse   78

A great tool to use is a "remote mouse." This enables you to advance slides on your laptop from anywhere in the room and gives you more freedom to interact with the audience. Most LCD projectors have a remote control feature that will advance your slides. If you don't have a remote mouse, a mouse with a long cord will at least give you some freedom of movement.

Video mute   79

Many LCD projectors have a "video mute" function that allows you to turn off the projected image using a remote control. This is a great tool to use when you want to direct attention to yourself, facilitate a discussion, or minimize the distraction of a slide showing on the screen.

80 *Function F7*

Most laptops have a function-F7 command that will turn off the projected image from your laptop (the "F" key may differ on some models). See "video mute" above for the benefits of this tool.

81 *Laser pointers*

I personally dislike laser pointers and I have found that most people find them distracting. If you insist on using a laser pointer, simply use the light to quickly direct the audience's attention to a specific location on your slide.

82 *How to avoid using a laser pointer*

The need to use a laser pointer typically indicates that your slides are too busy. Consider re-designing the slide to make better use of selective color to highlight locations on the slide. Or, use presentation software capabilities to circle, build, or otherwise highlight key points.

Microphones

83

Microphones often cause problems. Practice using a mike prior to a presentation. The easiest microphone to use is the lavaliere (lapel) mike that attaches to your clothing. Make sure you dress properly to allow the mike to easily attach and have a pocket for the transmitter (an especially important consideration for women).

Using video

84

You can incorporate video using a DVD player or with a laptop. If you are using a DVD, make sure the video segment is cued up in a way that minimizes the number of buttons you need to push to make it play. Short digital video clips are very effective when run through your laptop. Be sure your hardware and software are configured properly to run the video flawlessly.

85 *Video using a laptop*

Make sure you have the right computer, the right format, and the right audio capability to make the video effective. Preferably, use the same equipment during your presentation that you used in your practice session.

86 *Building graphics*

One advantage of computer-based presentations is that you can "build" content in order to maintain the audience's focus on a specific component of your slide. Be selective in using this feature. If you have a simple word slide, it can be distracting to build each line. Building is best when you are going to spend a minute or two on each segment built on the slide.

87 *Be selective with transitions*

PowerPoint allows you to use fancy transitions between slides. If you insist on using transitions such as a wipe, dissolve, or fly-in, pick one transition and stick with it. It is

annoying when a speaker tries to use every
transition available in a single presentation.

Don't overdo the bells and whistles 88

PowerPoint allows you to animate your slides,
have transitions between slides, and even add
sound each time you add information. Be very
selective in using these tools. Audiences are
more interested in what you say than in your
software skill.

PowerPoint 2007 89

The newest version of PowerPoint has some
great features that make it even easier to
develop professional visual aids, so it's worth
the upgrade. The Microsoft website provides
a tutorial to help you get started with this
updated tool.

90 *No need to be an expert*

While PowerPoint is a great tool, it can be very time-consuming if you try to try to use all its capabilities. You can literally spend hours playing with the design of a single word slide. You don't need to be an expert to put together presentations that will support your verbal message. Spend more time on the content and organization of your talk. Most likely, you are not getting paid to be a graphic designer.

Visual Aids

91 *Essential criteria*

Every visual aid must meet the following criteria:
1) it must be necessary (necessity);
2) it must be the best way to show a concept (clarity);
3) it must be simple (simplicity); and
4) it must be visible (visibility). Make sure each of your visual aids meet these criteria.

When to use them

Always ask, "Will a visual aid enhance the audience's understanding of what I am saying?" If the answer is yes, use a visual aid. There is no valid rule that will tell you how many visual aids you need for a presentation. Just focus on the needs of the audience and you will end up with the right amount.

Create your visual aids last

Speakers are tempted to jump on their computer and begin creating visual aids as soon as they are asked to give a presentation. But the creation of visual aids should be the last step in creating a presentation. Start creating visuals only after you have a defined purpose, a thorough understanding of the audience, and fully developed content. Remember, visual aids are only a tool—content is most important!

94 *Storyboarding*

Use storyboarding in drafting visual aids.
A storyboard is simply a visual representation
of your presentation outline. Sketch a visual
to match any main ideas or concepts in your
presentation. Create a visual story to match
your verbal content. It will save lots of time in
designing your final visual aids.

95 *Use PowerPoint to storyboard*

Use the "Outline" mode in PowerPoint as
a storyboarding guide. You can brainstorm
possible slides you will need and also record
notes that describe the possible visual
representations you may want to create.

96 *Try storyboarding software*

There are a number of software packages
available that let you storyboard and then
convert your thoughts to PowerPoint.
Just Google "storyboard." But remember,
don't let the software let you bypass the critical
steps of creating a clear objective
and thoroughly analyzing your listeners.

Keep it simple

97

Text slides are the most commonly used visual aid by most business professionals. Keep them simple. Try to have no more than five lines per slide and five words per line. This is a guideline, not a rule. But strive for simplicity.

Tease with titles

98

Consider using the title line of your slide to gain attention. For example, instead of writing "Objectives," write "What We Will Accomplish." Prompt some thinking from your audience and help keep them engaged.

Simple charts and graphs

99

The 5/5 guideline can also be applied to charts and graphs. Try to limit the number of bars on a bar chart to 5, and the number of lines on a graph to 5. This may not always be feasible, but try to keep charts and graphs as simple as possible.

100   *10 seconds or less*

A good visual aid should be understandable by an audience in 10 seconds or less without the speaker saying a word.

101   *Show less, say more*

This is a simple guideline to remember. It is better to have less information on a slide and elaborate on the content during your presentation, than to have a lot of information and only refer to selected content.
People will wonder why you did not talk about all the content!

102   *Be selective with color*

Color can help you focus attention on one element of your slide. Try to minimize the use of color so that it does not detract from your key points. Two to three colors per slide is usually sufficient.

Keep it simple

103

It is best to use "sans serif" type styles for any
visual aid. Examples of sans serif fonts are
Arial, Helvetica, Geneva, Tahoma, and Avant
Garde. These type styles are "blocky" and
project better.

Type size

104

Use the largest type sizes you can to insure
visibility. If possible, avoid any size less than
24 point.

Use icons instead of bullets

105

A simple way to improve a bulleted word slide
is to use symbolic icons instead of the boring
bullets. Choose icons that can enhance the
theme of your presentation.

106 *Use pictures*

Word slides can be more impactful if photos are used to support the bullets. For example, if you are talking about safety, show a photo of someone wearing proper safety equipment alongside the bullets.

107 *Color contrast*

A dark background with light text is best for computer projected slides. Color contrast is the key to visibility.

108 *Be careful with red*

Red is not clearly visible against the dark background preferred for computer-projected slides, yet many try to use this color for emphasis. Also, it's not a great idea to use red when discussing financial data.

The 6-foot test of visibility   109

If you are using a laptop, stand back six feet and test your slides for readability. Make your text and pictures as large as possible without sacrificing design.

Edit, edit, edit   110

Strive to be as concise and simple as possible with your visual aids. Keep editing and simplifying until you feel satisfied that each visual aid is on target.

Handouts   111

Handouts are visual aids. Handouts can be used for two purposes: 1) to help the audience follow your presentation; 2) to provide supplementary information or more detail about your presentation content. If your slides are properly designed, reproductions of three slides per page with space for notes is a great handout. Pass it out before you begin your presentation.

112 — *Slides vs. Handouts*

Many presenters create cluttered slides because they want the presentation to serve as a handout. There is nothing wrong with your handout having more information than the slides. Show less and say more!

113 — *Supplemental handouts*

A handout that provides supplementary information or additional details is best handed out AFTER your presentation. Avoid giving your audience the temptation to read while you present. Refer to the availability of an additional handout that you will provide after the presentation.

114 — *Use a professional*

You are the content expert, not the graphic designer. If you need a truly professional, high-tech presentation, plan ahead and hire a professional designer to polish the look of your graphics. You need to spend most of your time on the content, not the look.

Create an inventory 115

Whether you are part of a small business or
a major corporation, it is helpful to create
an inventory of slides and templates from
past presentations that can be accessed by
anyone in your organization. This makes it
easier for future presenters to locate graphics,
photos, charts, and other tools that may help
them support their messages and build more
professional presentations.

Microsoft resources 116

Microsoft provides a vast array of resources for
PowerPoint at http://office.microsoft.com.
You can find templates, clip art, animations
and much more. You will also find links
to other valuable websites that offer additional
resources. This website has a lot of stuff,
be careful not to be overwhelmed
and tempted to use more than you need for
a given presentation.

Using Your Eyes

How much is enough? 117

Effective eye contact is making a 2-second connection with a specific listener. One thousand one, one thousand two...that is enough. I have experimented with different intervals in many workshops and the consensus is that 2-second contact is perfect.

Get a response 118

Another way to gauge effective eye contact is to make contact with an individual until you get a non-verbal response—a nod, smile, or blinking of the eyes. Look for a signal that you have "connected" and then move on.

Avoiding the eyes 119

Some speakers have trouble making direct eye contact; they say it makes them lose their train of thought. Even in small groups you can avoid direct contact and still give the impression of

being confident and in control. Just look at
the bridge of the nose or the forehead instead
of the eyes; they won't be able to tell the
difference even at close range.

120 *Why make eye contact?*

In Western cultures, eye contact denotes
confidence, credibility, and comfort with your
subject. It is a powerful non-verbal gesture
that should be mastered by all speakers.

121 *Don't forget the corners*

Many speakers tend to make most of their eye
contact in the middle of the room and forget
about people who sit to the extreme right or
left. Be expansive with your eye contact and
draw in the complete room, don't forget the
people in the corners.

The eye contact magnets **122**

It doesn't matter how large the audience, speakers are drawn to the smiling faces and those who tend to show agreement with their talk through non-verbal gestures. Be aware of those who you are spending too much time making contact, don't forget the rest of the audience.

Eye contact and Q&A **123**

A common mistake during the Q&A session is the speaker devoting all of their eye contact to the person who asked the question. Remember, you still have an audience that needs to be involved in your response with both your verbal and non-verbal skills. Avoid the one-to-one dialogue during the Q&A session.

Barry F. Mitsch

124 *Eye contact in large groups —the zonal approach*

You can give the impression that you are making personal eye contact even with groups of 100 or more. Divide the audience into 6-8 zones and identify a friendly face in each zone. Then, make intermittent eye contact with the person in each zone as you give your presentation.

125 *Eye contact in large groups —the patterned approach*

Another approach is to follow a pattern when making eye contact in large groups. Follow a pattern that would look like a flattened infinity sign...move diagonally across the middle of the room from left to right, come up the right side, back across the room diagonally from right to left, up the left side...and slowly repeat.

126 *Eye contact for emphasis*

You can extend your eye contact on a specific individual if you want to make a point. Keeping eye contact for over 2 seconds with one

individual can grab their attention and help
you drive home a statement.

Be erratic with eye contact   127

In small groups, it's best to make "erratic" eye
contact. Try not to establish a predictable
pattern. It will help create some positive
tension that will help you maintain interest in
your presentation.

Try not to read   128

Audiences will tune out quickly if you lose eye
contact while reading too long from a book
or notes (see the section on notes and scripts
on page 77.

Notes   ---

Handling the Nerves

129   *Get out of your head*

Much of the nervousness created by public speaking comes from a fear of failure. We are worried about ourselves, not the audience. It is that voice in our head telling us all the negative things. When the focus becomes more on the audience and their needs, it is easier to get comfortable and start enjoying the experience. So, get out of your head...and into your heart. It's not about you and what you know; it's more about the audience and what you are sharing.

130   *Be prepared*

The best way to minimize nervousness is to be thoroughly prepared for the presentation. Be prepared, be relaxed, and be effective!

You are only human   131

Most people get nervous before speaking to
a group, regardless of the size. Realize that
the anxiety is normal! Mark Twain once said
there are only two types of speakers, those
that are nervous and those that are liars.

You don't look as nervous   132
as you feel

I have observed thousands of business
presentations over the years, both in
presentation skills classes and in day-to-day
business activities. Based on my observations,
I have calculated that 99.9% of the time
presenters do not *look* as nervous as they *feel*.
So, don't be so overly concerned
with that internal anxiety you feel. It is
something you feel inside, but is typically not
detectable outside.

Barry F. Mitsch

133 *Self talk*

A great technique to minimize the nerves is to use self talk. Every time that voice in your head starts to plant seeds of doubt, replace it with a positive self-talk statement. "I am a relaxed, confident speaker." Google "self talk" for a bunch of resources.

134 *Learn a relaxation technique*

I learned how to do "progressive relaxation" years ago and this technique has never failed me. Enter "relaxation" on the Google search engine and you will be able to access plenty of available relaxation methods. Find one that works and use it!

135 *Exercise*

I always exercise the night before a presentation. Take a walk, ride a bike, go to the gym...do something to "take the edge off" your anxiety.

Get a good night's sleep 136

No need to say more, this one is obvious.

Practice in the room 137

Practice always helps minimize anxiety.
It's best if you can do a dry run in the room
where you will be presenting. This helps you
become familiar with the environment and
also helps make any visualization techniques
more powerful.

Watch what you eat 138

I try to avoid spicy foods the night before
speaking and also eat a fairly bland breakfast
on the day of the presentation. When the
stomach begins to churn, I want to be sure
I can keep it under control. Pasta, oatmeal,
toast, and even grits seem to be good choices
for my "pre-game" meals.

139 *Curl your toes*

The "fight or flight" feeling we get during
a presentation can be difficult to control.
A technique that works for me—and has
worked for others—is to control the adrenalin
rush by rapidly curling your toes in your shoes.
It gives you an outlet for the energy and will
not be noticed by an audience (unless you are
wearing open-toed shoes).

140 *Watch the speed limit*

Slowing your rate of speech can help
you breath and also minimize the anxiety,
especially when beginning your presentation.
Try speaking a little slower at the outset of
your talk until you gain some confidence and
get in the flow.

141 *No excuses*

Avoid the temptation to make excuses.
Audiences don't care if you did not have a good
night's sleep, if you have a cold, or if you didn't
have time to prepare. Those kind of messages
take away from the impact of your presentation.

Meet and greet

142

One way to minimize your nervousness is to get to know the folks in your audience. Arrive early and "meet and greet" them as they fill the room. You will find they are just regular people who are looking forward to hearing what you have to say.

Tackling Questions

Three guidelines for handling questions

143

Just remember to be prepared, be brief, and be in control!

Timing of questions

144

The speaker can control when questions are asked by setting some ground rules. In your opening, state when you will allow questions:
1) after you have finished your presentation;
2) any time during the presentation; or
3) after main points in your presentation.

145   *Restating the question*

You only need to restate the question if
the room is large and you want to insure
that everyone has heard the question; or if
it is a complicated question that requires
you to restate and paraphrase to insure
understanding.

146   *Being prepared*

A great way to anticipate questions is to
conduct a practice presentation with some of
your colleagues. Ask them to help you prepare
for possible questions from the audience.

147   *Being brief*

Remember, you are answering a question,
not beginning a new presentation. Keep your
answers concise and focused on the question.
Resist the urge to pontificate or expound on
the topic—you risk generating more questions
that may keep you from achieving the objective
of your presentation.

Learn by observation

I have learned a lot about answering questions by watching White House, Pentagon, and State Department briefings. They are pros at staying on target and focused on a message. Tune into the news networks and learn from some skilled professionals.

Prompt questions

If you really want questions, prompt the questions by using a gesture. While asking, "Are there any questions?" walk toward the audience and raise your hand.

Use your non-verbal listening skills

When someone asks a question, demonstrate your interest by using non-verbal listening skills such as nodding, leaning towards them slightly, and making sincere eye contact.

151 *When you don't have the answer*

The worst thing you can do is give a wrong answer. It is best to defer, but don't apologize. Ask if you can get back with them with a thorough, accurate answer as soon as possible—and follow through on your promise!

152 *Deferring to a colleague*

If you don't have an answer, it may be appropriate to defer to a colleague who is prepared to answer the question. Plan ahead for this scenario by thoroughly anticipating the types of questions you may be asked. And be sure your colleague returns control of the meeting to you once they have answered.

153 *Ground rules help with interruptions*

If you have set ground rules in your opening as to when you will allow questions, you are in position to tactfully delay answering questions that result from interruptions. Simply restate the ground rule and ask if they can wait until the designated time.

Choose a strategy for answering **154**

If you are interrupted by a question, you have three options: 1) go ahead and answer; 2) partially answer and defer a full answer until later; or 3) defer completely. If a question supports a point you are making, it may be best to answer it completely.

Know your key points **155**

Knowing the key points and being comfortable with the flow of your presentation is essential for recovering from a question that interrupts your train of thought. Simply recap the main points and redirect the listeners to the specific point you were addressing prior to the interruption.

Maintain your professionalism **156**

Avoid confrontations with questioners if at all possible. Keep cool; the audience will respect your efforts to control your emotions.

157 *Concentrate on what, not who*

Very rarely are you challenged as an individual.
Rather, it is the content of your presentation
that is being questioned. Keep the discussion
focused on the content, not personalities.

158 *Keep everyone involved*

A common mistake made by many speakers
is turning the Q&A session into a dialogue with
a few people who are asking the questions.
If your answer to a question requires more than
two or three sentences, make sure to broaden
your eye contact and engage the entire group
as you would during your presentation.

159 *Remember your VIP's*

Every presentation has some VIP's—very
important points. Use the Q&A session to
bridge back to your points of emphasis.
For example, you are asked the question,
"Are you concerned about meeting next
quarter's budget?" Your answer ties back to
the fiscal controls that were emphasized in

your presentation, "No, the cost accountability measures we have introduced will make budget management much easier."

What do you mean? 160

A technique for diffusing a hostile question is to ask, "What do you mean?" This forces the questioner to restate the question and gives you time to settle yourself and avoid making a terse response.

Descending levels of agreement 161

A questioner may be more interested in sharing their own viewpoint. If you agree with their point of view, go ahead and say so. Or you may agree with parts of their point of view, or how things could be as they suggest. Finally, you can agree on their right to having a differing viewpoint. Look for the win-win solution.

Barry F. Mitsch

162

Offer to meet later

One way to diffuse a questioner who is belaboring a point and preventing you from proceeding with the rest of your presentation is to ask to meet them after the talk.
If you request this diplomatically, they will usually comply.

Notes

Using Your Body

Walk with confidence   163

From the very first instant that you stand up
and move to your presenting position, exude
confidence. Put a spring in your step!
Walk slightly faster than normal and portray
the image that you are ready to go.

The neutral position   164

A common question is "where do I put my
hands?" The best place to put your hands is in
a neutral position between your waist and your
shoulders. Place them lightly together, one on
top of the other or in a "steeple" configuration.
From neutral, your movements will be more
visible and have more meaning.

Smile, the forgotten gesture   165

One of the most powerful non-verbal gestures
is the smile. Yet many business presenters are
so serious that they forget about this simple

tool. When appropriate, use your smile to build rapport and show enthusiasm about your topic.

166 *Congruence*

Your verbal and non-verbal message needs to be congruent. If you can support a verbal with an effective non-verbal, your message will be even more powerful. If verbals and non-verbals do not agree, people tend to believe the non-verbal message.

167 *Nervous habits*

One of the best ways to identify nervous habits is to watch yourself on video. Habits such as rocking, swaying, tapping pointers, or using a repetitive gesture will become obvious, especially if you watch the tape in fast forward mode. Use video to minimize or eliminate bad habits.

Hands in pockets?

168

There is no rule that says you can't put your hands in your pockets. It can be a very effective gesture that indicates you are relaxed and casual. Just be selective in its use, and be sure to empty your pockets of any objects before you speak (especially coins and keys).

Stay square

169

It is best to stay "square" with the audience. Avoid turning your back, especially when pointing to information on a screen. Think of yourself as wearing a sweater with a number on the back. You don't want the audience to see the number.

Building gestures

170

You can build a repertoire of effective gestures through practice. Review your presentation and look for ways to enhance your message with your body. Practice using a gesture when you rehearse and incorporate the movement into your presentation.

171 — *Slow motion*

Gestures that are slow and sincere tend to have the greatest impact. Practice using slow motion gestures.

172 — *Meaningful movement*

Movement is a powerful tool for making transitions. A change in position while moving from one main point in your presentation to another will help signify a transition. The verbal message is supported by non-verbal movement.

173 — *Punctuate the point*

Movement towards an audience can help you emphasize a key point. Come out from behind a lectern, move away from your laptop, and move closer to the listeners when emphasizing a point. It will provide an element of change and a non-verbal exclamation point.

What to wear?

As a guideline, always be as well dressed as the best dressed person in the audience.

Be yourself

Some people find it very challenging to use their body and voice in ways that do not feel natural. The key is not just being yourself, but your BEST self. Many of the simple tips in this book can be used by anybody to improve their presentations. But remember to use only techniques that match your personality. Content is still the king, and everyone can develop great content that is well organized.

Notes

Videoconferencing

176 *Limitations*

Videoconferencing limits your body language and the rapport you can develop in a live presentation. Be aware that your voice becomes even more important in delivering a message. Use your vocal skills to have greater impact. Speak very clearly and be sure to articulate your words.

177 *Timing is important*

Videoconferences often have time constraints. Make sure your presentation is focused and practice enough to have the timing fairly accurate.

178 *Eye contact*

Eye contact during a videoconference is focused on the remote site. If you have a live audience in addition to those at remotes sites,

make occasional eye contact with the
live group with the majority being on the
remote site.

Visual aids & videoconferencing 179

Send copies of all of your visual aids and
additional handout material to the remote
site(s) ahead of time. Even if you are
using document cameras or other graphic
capabilities, audience members will find it
easier to read your visuals using a handout.

Watch what you wear 180

Wear solid colors to a videoconference with
colors in the pastel category being the best
choice. Depending on the bandwidth available
for the conference, stripes and patterns can
become distracting because of their distortion
when transmitted through video.

Presenting by Teleconference

181   *Use a headset*

It is important to keep your hands free so you can use a script if needed, take notes, and easily reach for any references or other materials during the call.

182   *Send out your handouts*

As with Tip 179, be sure everyone on the conference has the handout material at least one day before the conference.

183   *Clear your desk*

While it is impossible to keep teleconference participants from multi-tasking, you should do everything possible to keep yourself focused. Remove any possible distractions from your desk. Turn off your email, your cell phone, and even your computer if it is not needed for the conference call.

Barry F. Mitsch

MIND over *mutter*

Track participation

Creating interaction on a conference call can be challenging. Create a roster of participants on the call and track participation with check marks each time someone speaks. Ask questions or elicit comments from those you have not heard from. Use first names often to evoke participation.

Your voice is critical

You are limited to one mode of communication, so be very cognizant of your voice. Speak clearly, change speeds, change volume, use well placed pauses. Do everything possible to give your listeners some vocal change elements.

Notes

Computer conferencing

186   *Keep it simple*

Web conferencing programs have a wide array
of features. Only use the features that are
essential for your meeting and are tools that
you are confident in using.

187   *Load up your slides in advance*

Don't wait till the meeting to upload your slides
to the meeting platform. Make sure they are
loaded in advance and you have had a chance
to do a dry run.

188   *Ask questions and poll*

The polling feature on any platform is usually
one of the easiest to use. Simple polling
questions can keep your listeners engaged.
And remember to ask questions and evoke
responses from those who are reluctant
to participate.

Light backgrounds

Most graphic experts will recommend dark
backgrounds on projected slides. However,
a light background works best for computer
conferencing and viewing slides on a desktop
or laptop computer.

Notes & Scripts

Notes are a great tool

There is no rule that says you can't use notes in
a business presentation. Notes can add to your
confidence and help you stay focused. The key
to using notes is to make them a constructive,
not distracting, tool in the presentation.

Boil it down to basics

One way to prepare a presentation is to write
out your talk word for word. After reading your
presentation a few times, create notes from
the manuscript. Rehearse again using just the
notes. And then consolidate the notes even
further to a few key words.

192 *Practice with your final notes*

Always practice with the final version of your notes so you are familiar with the location of key words or visual prompts.

193 *5 x 7 Cards*

A great way to use notes is to boil down your main points and supporting key words to a few 5 x 7 cards. Simply arrange the cards on the table next to your laptop. Make the print large enough to see from a standing position, and refer to them as necessary.

194 *Flip charts*

Flip charts still have a useful role in casual presentations and small group settings. You can put your notes directly on a flip chart by lightly applying in pencil. No one will notice your notes; it can even make you appear to be a great artist as you skillfully trace an existing pencil drawing during your presentation.

Software notes

PowerPoint allows you to easily produce speaker notes. However, the default font for the notes is typically too small to read during a presentation. If you want to use this function, be sure to make the notes large enough and bold enough to read while you are presenting.

Speaking from a script

There may be the rare occasion when you are required to read from a prepared script (public relations response, legal response, corporate policy statements). Presentations can be effectively delivered from a script but you need to practice the delivery even more than in an extemporaneous talk. The mistake many people make is feeling that because they will be reading prepared text, they do not need to practice

Preparing a script

Use these guidelines when preparing a script: 1) double or triple space the text to make it easier to read; 2) always use upper and lower case letters; 3) number the pages; 4) only use the upper two-thirds of the paper for the text, this keeps you from having to look too far down.

198 *Choreograph the script*

Insert reminders to yourself to emphasize key words or phrases (underline, bold text), use slash marks in the text to remind yourself to slow down, and insert symbols as reminders to use a visual aid, refer to a document, or ask a question of the audience.

199 *Number the pages*

Always number the pages of your script or notes. You might drop them!

Notes

Checklists

Here are a few lists to help you plan and prepare your next presentation.

10 steps for creating a presentation

1) Identify a clear objective.
2) Analyze your listeners.
3) Brainstorm content.
4) Choose key points.
5) Organize and develop each key point.
6) Develop an opening.
7) Develop a closing.
8) Create transitions.
9) Design visual aids.
10) Practice the presentation.

10 questions to evaluate your visual aids

1) Are they necessary and add value to the message?
2) Are they designed to best express the message?
3) Are they simple?
4) Do word slides have 5 or less lines per slide?
5) Do word slides have 5 or less words per line?
6) Is there limited use of color?
7) Is the font size easily readable?
8) Is the font style sans serif?

9) Is there color contrast on slides?

10) Is there limited use of PowerPoint gimics?

10 points for evaluating a speaker

1) Clear opening, grabs attention, sets the stage
2) Body of the presentation well organized
3) Clear transitions between key points
4) Concise summary
5) Use of media appropriate
6) Natural gestures
7) Appropriate movement
8) Clear voice, use of vocal variety
9) Use of change elements
10) Limited physical and verbal distractions

10 ways to minimize the nerves

1) Prepare thoroughly
2) Practice in the room where you will speak
3) Exercise
4) Use self-talk
5) Learn a relaxation exercise
6) Visualize success
7) Get a good night's sleep
8) Minimize the caffeine
9) Meet and greet your audience
10) Focus on the audience's needs

10 ways to handle questions

1) Anticipate questions ahead of time
2) Be brief with answers
3) Set ground rules
4) Restate complicated questions
5) Restate questions with large audiences
6) Know your key points
7) Keep your cool
8) Defer
9) Watch the time
10) Avoid dialogues, include everyone

10 considerations for analyzing an audience

1) How many?
2) Technical expertise?
3) Room arrangement?
4) Male, female, mixed?
5) Expectations?
6) Previous experience with your topic?
7) Who is the decision maker?
8) Time constraints?
9) Preferred style of presentation?
10) Audio-visual or handout requirements?

10 *ways to practice a presentation*

1) Sub vocal practice at your desk
2) Quiet visualization
3) Private, vocal practice
4) Practice in front of a mirror
5) Practice with your last set of media
6) Audio-recorded practice
7) Private dress rehearsal
8) Practice with a coach
9) Video-recorded practice
10) Full dress rehearsal with an audience

Barry F. Mitsch

About the Author

Barry Mitsch has helped thousands of professionals with presentation style and content development over the past 20 years. His diverse background in business, science, corporate training, education, and community service helps him relate personally to almost any scenario where presentations are needed. He brings a unique practical perspective to his work that was born from a personal need to overcome his fear of speaking. Barry is Vice President of The Pyramid Resource Group, an award-winning corporate coaching and consulting company based in Cary, North Carolina. He can be reached at: barry@pyramidresource.com.

Colophon

Note from the Designer

Mind Over Mutter is set in typeface **National**,
the award-winning typeface designed by
Kris Sowersby in 2007. It was awarded the
Certificate of Excellence from the Type Designers
Club New York in 2008. It was chosen for its simple
san-serif nature with its unique and playful forms.
Since Mind Over Mutter is based on presentation
delivery, the typeface has a human charm that
turns simple tips into a conversation with mentor-
like qualities.

Brian M Johnson
RALEIGH, NORTH CAROLINA
October, 2009

Index

Barry F. Mitsch

Made in the USA
Charleston, SC
20 September 2016